Claudia Martin

ROCKS FOSSILS MINERALS AND GEMS

Quarto is the authority on a wide range of topics.
Quarto educates, entertains and enriches the lives of
our readers—enthusiasts and lovers of hands-on living.
www.quartoknows.com

Editor: Clare Hibbert
Designer: Dave Ball

© 2017 Quarto Publishing plc

This edition first published in 2018 by QEB Publishing,
an imprint of The Quarto Group.
6 Orchard Road, Suite 100
Lake Forest, CA 92630
T: +1 949 380 7510
F: +1 949 380 7575
www.QuartoKnows.com

A CIP record for this book is available from the Library of Congress.

ISBN 978 1 68297 310 3

Manufactured in Dongguan, China RD042018

9 8 7 6 5 4 3 2 1

MIX
Paper from
responsible sources
FSC® C101537

Contents

What is a Rock?

There are hundreds of types of rock. Some are hard, some are crumbly—and some are very strange!

This tower is made of a rock called sandstone. It is in Arizona.

ROCKY PLANET
Rock covers our planet. In some places bare rock is visible, but rock also lies under cities, soil, and oceans.

Rock families

There are three kinds of rock: igneous, sedimentary, and metamorphic. Each kind forms in a different way.

Igneous   Sedimentary   Metamorphic

Granite is an igneous rock that contains different colored minerals.

MINERAL MIXTURES

Rocks are mixtures of different minerals. Minerals grow in the ground or in water. They are solids.

5

Igneous
Rock

Deep inside the Earth is hot, runny rock called magma. When magma cools, it hardens to form igneous rock.

ERUPTION!

Some igneous rocks form when magma bursts onto the Earth's surface.

When magma erupts from a volcano, it is called lava. ▶

Obsidian forms when magma erupts from a volcano, then cools very fast.

Pumice forms when bubbly magma is thrown from a volcano.

Underground activity

Not all igneous rocks form at the surface. Gabbro is created when magma cools underground.

▲ Gabbro

The Giant's Causeway is made of slabs of basalt. The basalt formed when runny magma cooled and cracked.

ROUTE ACROSS THE SEA

According to legend, a giant built the Giant's Causeway in Northern Ireland. He needed to cross the sea to fight a Scottish giant.

Sedimentary Rock

Sedimentary rocks are made when pebbles, minerals, or dead animals and plants are pressed together.

Chalk is a soft, crumbly rock.

WHITE CLIFFS
Chalk is made from seashells which collected on the seabed. After millions of years, they hardened into rock.

LAYER ON LAYER

Look for layers of different materials in sedimentary rocks. Sandstone is pressed sand. Mudstone and shale are pressed mud.

◄ These stripes are layers of sandstone and mudstone.

ON THE MOVE

Earth is covered by massive, slow-moving plates of rock. They push land together or pull it apart. What was once seabed can end up far inland.

▼ These pointed pieces of limestone formed from shells and corals. The area is now a desert!

Metamorphic
Rock

Any rock can change into metamorphic rock. All it takes is great heat or pressure.

MOVING PLATES

Rock sometimes comes under pressure from the movement of Earth's plates. This can squash or fold the rock.

This metamorphic rock, schist, has been bent and folded.

Slate is shale that has been pressed. Shale is a sedimentary rock made from mud.

HEATING UP

Many metamorphic rocks are made when rocks get very hot. This can happen deep inside the Earth.

The metamorphic rock marble is limestone that has been heated. Its swirling colors are made by minerals in the limestone.

Gemstones

Some metamorphic rocks contain secrets. Precious gems can grow from minerals trapped in the super-hot rock.

This ruby formed inside a slab of marble.

Amazing
Patterns

Some rocks are striped or lumpy. The patterns tell us how the rocks were made.

BRILLIANT BANDS
Stripes can form in metamorphic rocks. It happens when pressing, sliding, or heat separate the different minerals in the rock.

Gneiss has stripes of dark and light minerals.

UNUSUAL SURFACES
Sedimentary rocks often form with lumps and bumps.

◄ Mineral grains called ooliths settled on this limestone.

Conglomerate is mudstone or sandstone with pebbles trapped in it. ►

ANCIENT LIFE FORMS
Some sedimentary rocks are patterned with fossils.

Ferns were preserved in this sandstone. ◄

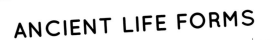

Rainbow mountains

The striped mountains in Danxia, China, are made of different-colored sandstones. The layers were pushed and turned by the Earth's plates.

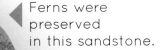

Strange **Shapes**

Wind, rain, and rivers can rub rocks into weird shapes. This is called erosion.

AMAZING ARCHES
Arches can form when wind and water wear away soft rock. Harder rock is left behind.

Carved canyon

The Grand Canyon in Arizona is 277 miles (446 km) long. It was worn away by the Colorado River.

STUNNING STACKS

Waves and wind can wear cliffs into towers called stacks. The Twelve Apostles are limestone stacks off the coast of Australia.

Only eight of the Twelve Apostles are left.

FAIRY CHIMNEYS

Odd pillars of rock are sometimes called fairy chimneys or hoodoos.

15

A sandstone arch in Utah

Fairy chimneys in central Turkey

Hoodoos in Utah

Deep **Caves**

Deep, dark caves can be found underground.
They are worn away by water.

DISSOLVING ROCK

When rainwater or water from an underground river soaks into limestone, the rock dissolves. Tiny grains of rock mix with the water and are carried away.

These limestone caves are in Slovenia. ▶

Slow growers

Even the fastest stalactites form quite slowly—just 1/8 inch (3 mm) per year!

Some minerals dangle from the ceiling as stalactites.

DRIP, DRIP

Water containing the dissolved minerals drips into the cave. It leaves some minerals behind.

Some minerals collect below a dripping stalactite. They build up into towers called stalagmites.

Useful **Rock**

Humans have used rocks for thousands of years. There are useful rocks everywhere!

STONE AGE
Before people knew how to work with metal, they used hard rocks to make weapons and tools.

BUILDING BLOCKS
Strong, sturdy rock can create beautiful buildings.

India's Taj Mahal is built from marble.

Stone Age people carved arrowheads from rock.

FOSSIL FUEL

Coal is a sedimentary rock made of plants which died millions of years ago.

▲ Gravel helps water to drain away.

▲ Coal is burned as a fuel.

GREAT GRAVEL

Pieces of rock, called gravel, are used to build roads.

Deepest mine

Miners dig into rocks to find useful minerals, such as gold and salt. The deepest mines go more than 2 miles (3.2 km) into the ground.

Rock **Art**

Rocks can be turned into amazing art.
They can be carved, molded, or painted.

SUPER SAND

Sand is found on beaches and in deserts, where waves or wind break rock into little pieces.

Buddhist monks used colored sand to make this mandala.

STONE CARVING

It takes years of practice to carve stone into statues or furniture.

▼ This sculptor is using a chisel to carve stone.

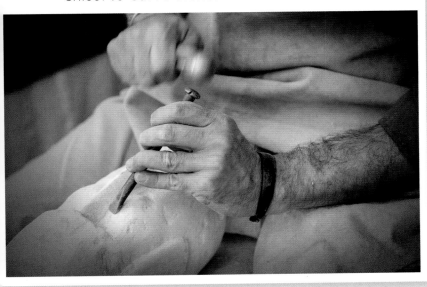

Cave paintings

Around 40,000 years ago, humans started to paint the walls of caves. They often drew the animals they hunted.

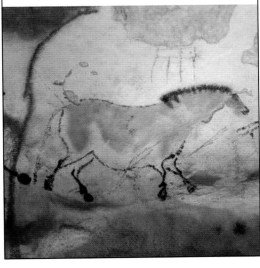

▲ Lascaux Cave, France

▼ After clay is shaped, it can be hardened by heating it.

PERFECT POTS

Clay is a soft rock. It was formed from plants and minerals mixed with water.

What is a Fossil?

Fossils are the remains of animals and plants that lived thousands or even millions of years ago.

FOUND IN ROCKS

Fossils are usually found in rocks. Paleontologists are scientists who dig up fossils—very carefully!

◀ Paleontologists find and study fossils.

LOOK INTO THE PAST

Over millions of years, Earth's animals and plants have slowly changed. Fossils show us what animals and plants looked like long ago.

Without fossils, we would not know that dinosaurs existed! ▼

▲ These bacteria are the oldest-known fossils.

How Fossils Form

Most animals and plants rot away after they die. Luckily, when something dies in a suitable spot, a fossil can form.

BODY FOSSILS

A body fossil is the remains of an animal's body or a plant. It can form when the remains are buried in sand or mud. Over time, the sand or mud turn to stone—and so do any hard parts of the animal or plant, such as bones, shells, teeth, or bark.

Dragon bones?

For thousands of years, people found dinosaur fossils but did not know what they were. The ancient Chinese thought they were dragon bones.

This body fossil is *Pterodactylus*, a flying reptile that lived 150 million years ago.

TRACE FOSSILS

A trace fossil is not a plant or animal's body. It is a mark or trace left by a living thing. Trace fossils include footprints, burrows, and poop!

This fossilized dinosaur poop has hardened into rock.

Hunting for Fossils

Anyone can go looking for fossils.
Where are the best places to look?

▲ These sandstone cliffs in England contain fossils from around 200 million years ago.

FOSSIL HOTSPOTS

You often find fossils in sedimentary rock, such as sandstone and chalk. These rocks formed from layers of sand or mud.

This dinosaur skull was found in sandstone in Utah. ▶

JIGSAW PUZZLE

When a paleontologist finds a fossil, they cut it carefully out of the rock. Back at the laboratory, they clean it and piece together broken parts.

◀ A paleontologist cleans a *Triceratops*'s horn.

Get a move on!

Paleontologists examine bones for signs of how they were attached to muscles. This gives clues about how the animal moved.

Reconstruction of a *T. rex*'s leg ▶

Sea **Creatures**

Life on Earth began in the sea. Some of the oldest fossils we have found are of sea creatures.

AMAZING AMMONITES

Ammonites looked like squid inside spiral-shaped shells.

Ammonites are one of the easiest fossils to find. ▶

TOP TRILOBITES

Trilobites were soft-bodied creatures with a hard covering, like a crab.

▲ Trilobites looked a bit like woodlice.

DOLPHIN-SHAPED

Icthyosaurs were swimming reptiles. They had streamlined bodies, like dolphins.

Icthyosaurs lived from 250 to 90 million years ago. ▲

FISH FOSSILS

The first fish appeared 530 million years ago.

▲ This spiny fish lived 40 million years ago.

Living fossil

People thought the coelacanth (say 'see-lo-canth') fish died out with the dinosaurs. Then, in 1938, live ones were discovered!

Discovering **Dinosaurs**

The dinosaurs were an amazing group of reptiles. They first walked the Earth 230 million years ago.

The sauropods were huge plant-eating dinosaurs with long necks.

FUNNY WALK

Like other reptiles, dinosaurs breathed air, had leathery skins, and laid eggs. Unlike other reptiles, dinosaurs walked with their legs straight under their bodies, not sprawled out to the sides.

Fossilized dinosaur skin

Dinosaur tracks in Colorado

DIFFERENT DIETS

Some dinosaurs were hunters who ate other dinosaurs and animals for food. Others fed on plants.

Meat-eating *T. rex*'s teeth were around 12 inches (30 cm) long.

Terrible lizards

Dinosaur means "terrible lizard" in Greek. The biggest meat-eaters, such as Allosaurus (below), had huge, powerful jaws.

▲ This fossilized egg is from *Hadrosaurus*, a plant-eating dinosaur.

Strange and
Extinct

Dinosaurs are not the only strange animals that once roamed the Earth. Fossils have taught us about others.

EARLY ELEPHANTS

Mammoths had trunks and were related to today's elephants. They died out 4,500 years ago.

Mammoth skeleton ▶

SLIMY LIZARD

Seymouria looked like a lizard, but it was an amphibian, like a frog. It lived in water when young, then crawled onto land as an adult.

▲ *Seymouria* lived 280 million years ago.

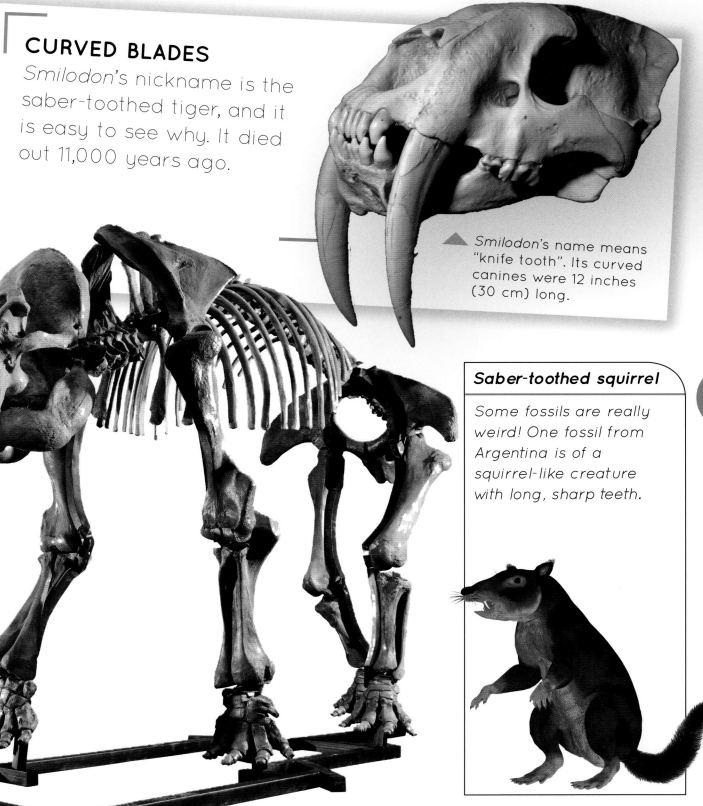

CURVED BLADES

Smilodon's nickname is the saber-toothed tiger, and it is easy to see why. It died out 11,000 years ago.

▲ *Smilodon*'s name means "knife tooth". Its curved canines were 12 inches (30 cm) long.

Saber-toothed squirrel

Some fossils are really weird! One fossil from Argentina is of a squirrel-like creature with long, sharp teeth.

Wonderful
Wings

When did animals first flap through the air? Fossils can give us the answer!

FLUTTERING INSECTS

Insects were the earliest flying animals. The oldest fossils of winged insects are 400 million years old.

Millions of years ago, this gnat got stuck in resin that oozed from a tree. The resin slowly hardened into stone called amber.

Dragonflies have been darting around for 325 million years.

WINGED DINOSAURS

Over millions of years, dinosaurs evolved (changed). By 150 million years ago, some dinosaurs had wings.

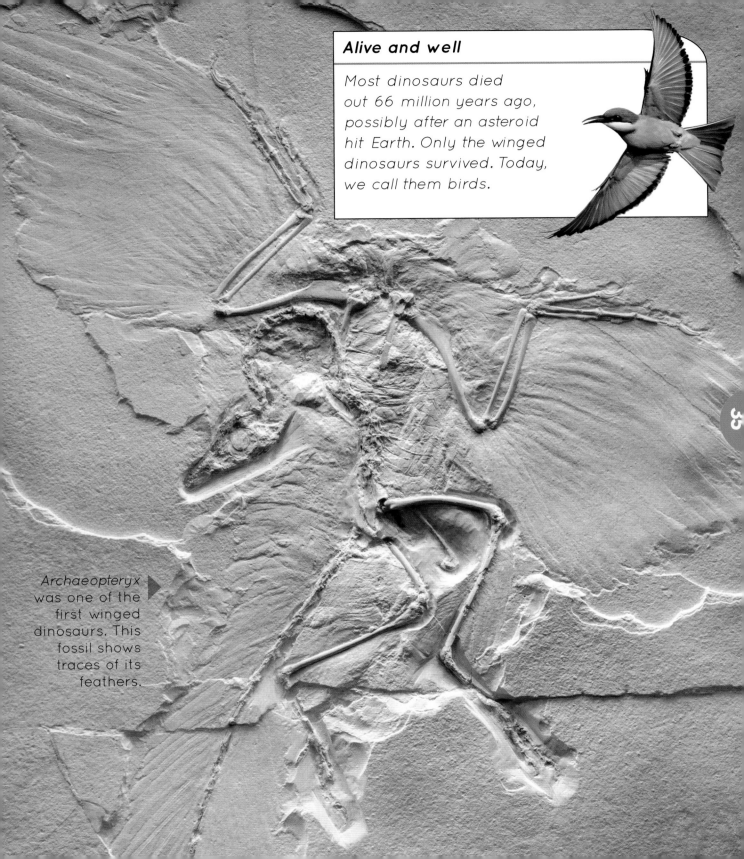

Alive and well

Most dinosaurs died out 66 million years ago, possibly after an asteroid hit Earth. Only the winged dinosaurs survived. Today, we call them birds.

Archaeopteryx was one of the first winged dinosaurs. This fossil shows traces of its feathers.

Precious
Plants

Some of the most beautiful fossils are plants. Look out for fossilized leaves, stems, trunks, and even petals.

COMPLETELY PETRIFIED

Petrified means "turned to rock." Wood can turn to rock when it is buried under sand or mud. Over time, minerals grow in the wood, replacing its living material with rock.

Petrified tree stumps in Arizona

LOVELY LEAVES

Cycads are plants with large, stiff leaves. Fossils tell us that they have hardly changed in the last 150 million years.

◄ Fossilized cycad leaves

Today cycads usually grow in hot countries ►

FAINT FLOWER

Fossilized flowers are very rare because petals are so delicate.

This flower fossil is 35 million years old.

Watch your step!

The nearest fossil may be closer than you think. Look down! Paving stones can contain fossilized ferns.

What is a Mineral?

Minerals are solids that grow in the ground or in water. There are around 5,000 different minerals.

BUILDING BLOCKS
Minerals are made of pure, simple substances called elements. There are more than 100 elements. Everything on Earth is made up of elements.

This mineral, quartz, is made from the elements silicon and oxygen.

MINERAL MIX

Some minerals grow when different elements join together. Others contain just one element.

Rhodocrosite is a mineral made from the elements carbon, oxygen, and manganese.

Rocky mix-up

Rocks are mixtures of minerals. The main mineral in the rock quartzite is quartz.

Diamond is a mineral made from only one element: carbon.

How Minerals Grow

Minerals grow when the tiniest parts of an element, called atoms, stick to other atoms.

GROWING UNDERGROUND

Beneath the Earth's surface is hot, runny rock called magma. When the magma cools, atoms start to stick together.

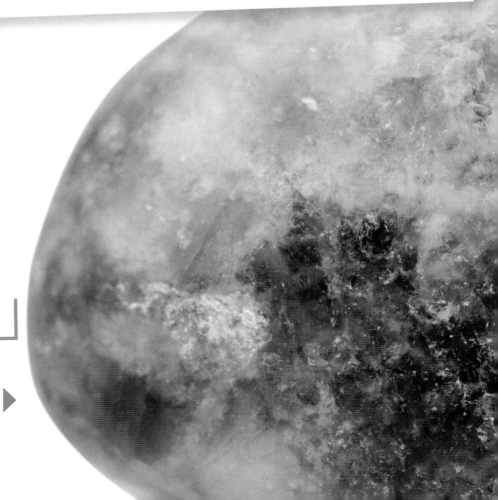

Lepidolite grows in cooling magma. It is made from atoms of silicon, oxygen, potassium, and other elements.

GROWING IN WATER

Water often has atoms of different elements in it. When water evaporates (floats away as a gas), those atoms are left behind.

Gypsum grows when water evaporates and leaves behind calcium and sulfur.

Rare or not?

Common minerals such as quartz are made from elements which are common in rocks or water. Other minerals, such as brookite, are very rare.

This brookite crystal formed in quartz.

Amazing **Crystals**

If a mineral has plenty of room, it grows in a regular shape called a crystal.

◄ Epidote crystals form tall, slanted rectangles.

REPEATING PATTERN

When a mineral starts to form, its atoms stick to each other in a special pattern. If nothing interrupts the growing mineral, it continues building the same pattern.

Scolecite often grows as groups of thin needles. ►

SIGNATURE SHAPE

You can identify minerals by the shape of their crystals.

Vanadinite crystals form six-sided shapes called hexagons.

▲ Pyrite crystals can form cubes.

▲ Amazonite crystals grow into wedge shapes.

FLOWERY POMPOMS

In damp caves, aragonite crystals can make flower-like shapes. They form when dripping water contains calcium and carbon.

Bright and
Beautiful

Some minerals have bright colors.
Different elements make different colors.

MULTICOLORED
MINERAL

Elbaite comes in every
color of the rainbow.
One crystal can be
more than one color.

Red and green
elbaite crystals
are called
"watermelon."

GORGEOUS GEMS

Some beautifully colored, hard minerals are used to decorate jewelry. They are known as gemstones.

Aquamarine is a beryl crystal, made sea-blue by traces of iron.

A ruby is a crystal of the mineral corundum, tinted red by the element chromium.

Citrine is a quartz crystal, yellowed with a little iron.

Paint palette

In the past, some minerals were ground to make colorful paint. Azurite made a deep blue.

Powdered azurite

Shining **Metals**

Metals are found in rocks. They are minerals too! Pure metals contain just one element.

METALLIC FEATURES

Metals are shiny, strong, and melt when heated. They are used to make jewelry, coins, and machinery.

These gold crystals formed on a piece of quartz.

Copper crystals grow in branching clusters.

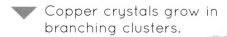

Most expensive

The metal rhodium is far more expensive than gold. It is used in special machines that cut down the pollution given out by cars.

Catalytic converters reduce car pollution. ▶

AWESOME ORES

Some minerals contain metals mixed with other elements. These minerals are called ores. They are mined and then heated to remove the useful metal.

▲ The mineral magnetite contains the metal iron.

The mineral sphalerite is ▶ an ore of the metal zinc.

Strange and **Powerful**

Some minerals behave very strangely. You could say they have super powers!

GLOWING AND FADING

A few minerals do odd things when they are exposed to light. Autunite glows in the dark after it has soaked up ultraviolet light.

Autunite

Proustite is red until it is put in sunlight. Then it turns dark.

TICK TOCK

If you pass electricity through quartz, it shakes at a regular pace. Many watches contain a tiny quartz crystal, which keeps them ticking evenly.

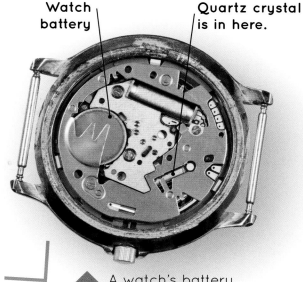

Watch battery

Quartz crystal is in here.

▲ A watch's battery sends electricity to a quartz crystal.

Quartz crystal

Giant gypsum

The biggest mineral crystals ever discovered were 36 feet (11 m) long. The gypsum crystals grew in a hot, wet cave in Mexico.

Record-breaking gypsum crystals ▶

Most **Deadly**

Do not be deceived by the beauty of these minerals. They could be killers!

CAUTION!

Minerals can be dangerous if they contain poisonous elements. Orpiment contains arsenic, which was used to kill rats and insects.

Cinnabar contains poisonous mercury.

Stibnite used to be shaped into knives and forks, until people realized it was poisonous.

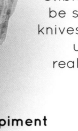

Orpiment

KILLER KOHL

The ancient Egyptians used the mineral galena to make dark eyeliner called kohl. Galena contains lead, which can damage the brain if swallowed.

The Egyptians made eye makeup with minerals.

Galena

RADIOACTIVE

Minerals that contain the element uranium are radioactive. This means they release energy that can damage human bodies.

This mineral, uranophane, contains radioactive uranium.

Hunting for
Minerals

Minerals are dug out of the ground by miners. You can also look for them yourself.

LUCKY BREAK

The best places to hunt for minerals are where rocks are broken open. Running water and waves break open rocks on beaches and riverbeds.

This lucky collector has found quartz.

MINING

Metals and gemstones are just some of the minerals that are mined from the ground.

▼ These underground workers are mining gold.

Prehistoric mine

One of the world's oldest mines is in Swaziland, Africa. More than 40,000 years ago, miners there dug up hematite to make red paint.

Useful **Minerals**

There are lots of useful minerals. You can find them in factories, fields, homes, and food!

LOOKING GOOD
The mineral fluorite is used in toothpaste to make teeth white and strong. Mica adds shine to lipsticks and nail polish.

◀ Fluorite helps to stop tooth decay.

Gleaming mica in a mica mine ▶

TRULY TASTY

Farmers fertilize their crops with phosphorus, a mineral found in apatite. Food itself is seasoned with salt, a mineral called halite.

Halite is dug from mines or collected from evaporated seawater.

Apatite contains phosphorus, which helps plants grow.

GETTING CREATIVE

Minerals are used by artists in paints and pencils. Craftworkers such as potters or glassblowers use them too.

Feldspar is used to make glass and pottery.

Pencil "lead" is not really the metal lead. It is the soft mineral graphite.

What is a
Gemstone?

A gemstone is a pretty mineral or rock which is used to make jewelry.

Lemon quartz

Rose quartz

MINERALS
Most gemstones are minerals. They form underground when hot, liquid rock from inside the Earth cools down.

Quartz

Amethyst

Green amethyst

Citrine

Smoky quartz

CRYSTAL GEMS

As a mineral grows, it forms regular shapes called crystals. Only hard, beautiful minerals are used as gems.

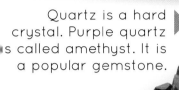

Quartz is a hard crystal. Purple quartz is called amethyst. It is a popular gemstone.

Using gemstones

Gemstones need to be hard. Nobody would buy a jewel which could easily crack!

This gemstone jewelry includes amethysts, green malachite, and amber.

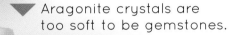

Aragonite crystals are too soft to be gemstones.

Colorful
Jewels

Some gemstones are brightly colored. Gems take on their color as they form in the ground.

Rough ruby

Rough sapphire

RED AND BLUE

Rubies and sapphires are both made from the same mineral, corundum. On its own, corundum has no color. But if chemical elements mix with it, it's a different story.

Polished

This is a ruby. It is red because the element chromium got into the crystal as it was forming.

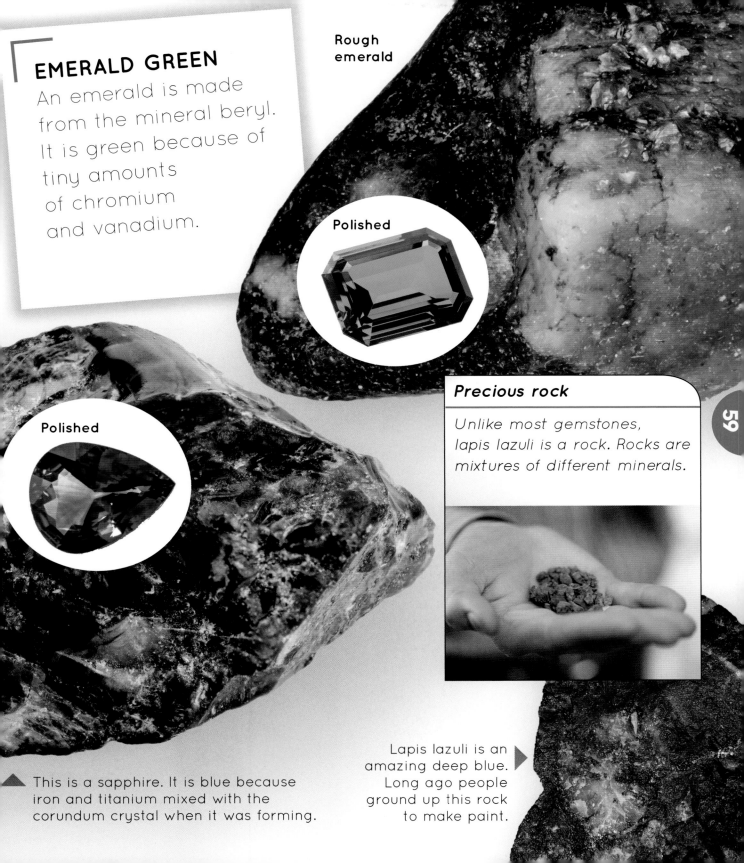

EMERALD GREEN

An emerald is made from the mineral beryl. It is green because of tiny amounts of chromium and vanadium.

Rough emerald

Polished

Polished

Precious rock

Unlike most gemstones, lapis lazuli is a rock. Rocks are mixtures of different minerals.

▲ This is a sapphire. It is blue because iron and titanium mixed with the corundum crystal when it was forming.

Lapis lazuli is an amazing deep blue. Long ago people ground up this rock to make paint. ▶

Dazzling
Diamonds

Diamonds are the hardest minerals.
They are made deep inside the Earth.

A pure diamond
has no color. ▶

This diamond has
not been shaped
or polished yet. ▶

PURE

Diamonds are made of the element carbon. Elements are pure materials that are the building blocks for everything on Earth. There are more than 100 elements.

ANCIENT GEM

All diamonds formed at least one billion years ago. They were made inside rocks that contained carbon. Carbon has to get extremely hot before it forms a diamond.

Pure gold is one of the elements. ▶

Sharp as a knife

Diamonds are so hard that they can cut other materials. They are used in drills for cutting rock or metal.

The tip of this drill ▲ for polishing metal is made of diamond.

Precious
Patterns

Some gemstones are prized because of their stripes, spots, or other amazing patterns.

BLUE STRIPES

Agate forms in an empty pocket inside a rock. It grows slowly, layer by layer. Different colors are made as the temperature or pressure changes.

▼ Malachite is a banded mineral with a bright green color.

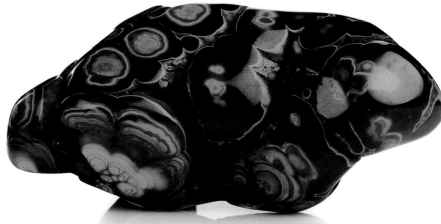

Agate is made from the mineral quartz. ▶

Ball of jasper ▶

JASPER
Like agate, jasper is made from quartz. Unlike agate, jasper is opaque, which means it cannot be seen through.

▼ This spotted rock is named Dalmatian jasper, after the dog.

WILD STRIPES
Tiger's eye is a rock made of quartz and other minerals. The quartz crystals have grown in striped rows.

Tiger's eye reflects the light like a cat's eye. ▶

Hiding
Inside

Gemstones can be hidden in surprising places—inside dull-looking stones, other gemstones, and even shells!

SECRET MINERALS

On the outside, a geode looks like an ordinary rock. Break it open, and you will discover crystals have grown inside!

This geode contains amethyst crystals. ▶

MINERALS INSIDE MINERALS

A mineral can grow around the crystals of another mineral.

▼ A mineral called rutile is trapped inside these quartz crystals.

◄ A star sapphire contains crystals of rutile that form a starlike pattern.

STICKY SAP

Amber is a clear, golden gemstone. It forms from sticky resin that oozed from trees millions of years ago.

Pacific pearls

Pearls form inside the shells of oysters or other shellfish. They are iridescent, which means they shimmer and seem to change color.

Found in
the Ground

Most gemstones are found inside rocks in the ground. They have to be dug up or blasted out.

▼ This huge emerald is from an underground mine in Colombia.

MINING
Some gemstones are close to the surface. Miners dig an open pit or hole and check the rocks for gems. Other gemstones are deep underground. Miners dig shafts and tunnels to reach them.

BOOM!

Sometimes miners blast rocks apart with big explosions.

An explosion in an open-pit diamond mine ▶

ROUGH GEMSTONES

When gemstones come out of the ground, they are called "rough" gemstones. They may be jagged, dull, or stuck in other rocks.

From the lab

Synthetic gems do not come from the ground. Chemists make them! They mix elements at the right temperature and pressure.

Cubic zirconia, a ▲ lab-created "diamond"

Rough garnet

Rough diamond

Rare and **Strange**

Some gemstones are very rare and expensive. Others create special effects.

BLACK OPALS

Opals come in every color of the rainbow, but black ones are the rarest. Most of them come from one town in Australia: Lightning Ridge.

All opals seem to be flecked with flickering colors.

RARE BEYOND COMPARE

Tanzanite is a rare gemstone that is found in one area of Tanzania, Africa. Painite is another rare gem.

Tanzanite is purply-blue. ▲

DOUBLE VISION

Iceland spar is see-through. When you look through it, you see two of everything!

Iceland spar bends and divides light.

◄ Fewer than 100 painite crystals ▲ have ever been found!

Diamonds from space

Some diamonds do not form underground. They fall to Earth from space, inside rocks called meteorites.

Meteorite

COLOR CHANGE

In sunlight, alexandrite looks green or yellow. In electric light, it looks purple, pink, or red.

◄ Alexandrite in natural light

◄ Alexandrite in artificial light

69

Cutting and
Polishing

Before gemstones are put into jewelry, they are cut and polished. This shows off the stones' color or sparkle.

A labradorite cabochon

COLORFUL CABOCHON
An opaque gemstone is often cut into a smooth, domed shape called a cabochon. It shows off the gemstone's colors and patterns.

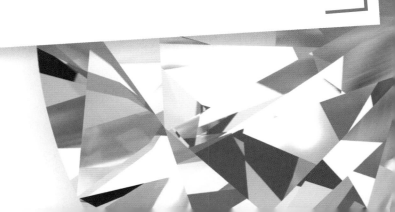
An opal cabochon

SPARKLING SHAPE

Translucent or see-through gemstones are often cut to have many small, flat windows called facets. These bounce the light around for extra sparkle.

A machine polishes each facet.

Diamonds can be cut into many different, faceted shapes.

Many-sided

The more facets a diamond has, the sparklier it seems. Diamonds can be cut with up to 144 facets.

Famous
Jewels

Gems can make quite a name for themselves—these jewels are world-famous!

MOST FAMOUS

The Crown Jewels belong to the UK's kings and queens. The 13 crowns hold many precious gems. The collection also includes a scepter decorated with the world's largest cut clear diamond, the Cullinan I.

The Imperial State Crown

Black Prince's Ruby

Cullinan II diamond

RECORD PRICE
In 2016, the Oppenheimer Blue diamond became the most expensive gemstone. It sold for $57,500,000.

The Murat Tiara
This tiara of diamonds and pearls was made as a wedding gift in 1920. In 2012 it sold for $3,864,318.

BIGGEST ROBBERY
One of the world's biggest robberies took place in 2015 in London, UK. The robbers made off with jewels and other loot worth more than $300,000,000.

▼ The robbers blasted open this door to reach the valuables.

ENORMOUS EMERALDS
The biggest emeralds come from Brazil's Bahia region. One weighed 750 pounds (341 kg)– as much as four men.

An emerald from Bahia, Brazil ▶

Guide

ROCKS

BASALT

Type: Igneous
Description: Dark gray and hard

CHALK

Type: Sedimentary
Description: White, soft, and crumbly

CLAY

Type: Sedimentary
Description: White to brownish-orange; soft when wet

COAL

Type: Sedimentary
Description: Brown or black; easy to burn

CONGLOMERATE

Type: Sedimentary
Description: Rounded pebbles cemented into sandstone or mudstone

GRANITE
Type: Igneous
Description: Gray or pinkish with grains of colored minerals

LIMESTONE

Type: Sedimentary
Description: Gray to yellowish; slowly dissolves in rainwater

MARBLE

Type: Metamorphic
Description: White or pink to blue, green, or black; can have swirling patterns

OBSIDIAN

Type: Igneous
Description: Dark, very hard and shiny

PUMICE

Type: Igneous
Description: Pale, full of holes, and lightweight

SANDSTONE

Type: Sedimentary
Description: Sand-colored, from white to black; rough and grainy

SLATE

Type: Metamorphic
Description: Usually gray; easy to split into flat sheets

FOSSILS

AMBER

Description: Hardened tree resin that can contain minibeasts
Where to find: Fairly common in rocks or on beaches

AMMONITE

Description: Spiral shell (or a mold of the shell's insides)
Where to find: Fairly common on cliffs and beaches

COPROLITE

Description: Animal poop
Where to find: Very rare, in rocks worldwide

DINOSAUR
Description: Bones, teeth, eggs, or marks left by skin or feathers
Where to find: Rare, in deserts and cliffs

FOOTPRINT
Description: The shape of an animal's foot, pressed into mud
Where to find: Rare, where rock is worn away by waves or cut away by mining or construction

MAMMOTH
Description: Bones, tusks, and teeth of elephantlike animals
Where to find: Rare, in Africa, Asia, Europe, and North America

PETRIFIED WOOD
Description: Wood that has turned to rock
Where to find: Fairly common worldwide

TRILOBITE
Description: Body parts of shelled sea creatures (or a mold of their shape)
Where to find: Common fossil in cliffs and quarries

MINERALS

ARAGONITE
Color: Usually white, but may be colored
Where to find: In caves and around hot springs

AZURITE
Color: Bright blue
Where to find: In rocks close to the metal copper

CINNABAR
Color: Red
Where to find: In rocks close to volcanoes

DIAMOND
Color: Usually colorless
Where to find: Deep underground; brought nearer to the surface by moving magma

EPIDOTE
Color: Usually green
Where to find: In rock that has been heated

GOLD
Color: Golden yellow
Where to find: In rocks, often mixed with silver; sometimes in small flakes in streams

GYPSUM
Color: Usually colorless or pale
Where to find: In limestone and clay caves

MAGNETITE
Color: Gray to black
Where to find: In rock that has been heated

PYRITE
Color: Yellow to gray
Where to find: In a wide range of rocks

QUARTZ
Color: Colorless when pure; may be any color
Where to find: Common in many rocks and pebbles

GEMS

AGATE
Type: Mineral
Appearance: Translucent; stripes of color ranging from white and yellow to blue, red, and green

AMBER
Type: Hardened resin
Appearance: Translucent; ranging from yellow to red

AMETHYST
Type: Mineral
Appearance: Transparent to translucent; purple

DIAMOND
Type: Mineral
Appearance: Usually transparent and colorless; may be colored

EMERALD
Type: Mineral
Appearance: Transparent to translucent; green

JASPER
Type: Mineral
Appearance: Opaque; stripes of brown, yellow, red, green, or blue

LAPIS LAZULI
Type: Rock
Appearance: Opaque; blue

OPAL
Type: Similar to a mineral, but not a crystal
Appearance: Transparent to opaque; ranges from white to black, to rainbow colors

RUBY
Type: Mineral
Appearance: Transparent to translucent; red

SAPPHIRE
Type: Mineral
Appearance: Transparent to translucent; usually blue, but may be any color except red

Glossary

asteroid A rock that travels in space, moving around the Sun.

atom The smallest parts of an element that can exist by themselves.

bacteria Tiny, simple living things, some of which cause disease.

body fossil The hardened remains of the body of a dead animal or plant.

cabochon A polished, rounded gemstone.

crystal The regular shape that a mineral forms as it grows.

dinosaur One of a group of reptiles that lived on land from 230 to 66 million years ago.

dissolves Mixes in with water or another liquid.

element A pure, basic substance.

erosion Wearing away by wind, water, or ice.

evaporate Turn from a liquid into a gas.

evolved Changed very slowly, over thousands of years.

extinct Died out.

facet A small, flat surface.

fossil The remains of an animal or plant that lived long ago, pressed into rock or turned into rock.

fuel A material that is burned to make heat.

gemstone A beautiful and hard mineral or rock that is used in jewelry.

geode A hollow rock that contains minerals.

hominin A modern human, an early human, or a humanlike creature.

igneous rock Rock formed when magma cools down and hardens.

iridescent Shimmering with different colors.

magma Hot, runny rock that lies beneath Earth's surface of cool, hardened rock.

mandala A round picture that represents the universe for Hindus or Buddhists.

metal A solid that is usually hard and shiny. Metal melts when it is heated and can also be hammered into new shapes.

metamorphic rock Rock formed when any type of rock is changed by heat or pressure.

meteorite A piece of rock or metal that has fallen to Earth from space.

mineral A solid formed in the ground or in water. Each mineral is a mix of elements.

opaque Not able to be seen through.

ore A rock or mineral that contains a useful metal.

paleontologist A scientist who studies fossils.

plate One of the giant slabs of rock that make up the surface of the Earth.

pollution Damage to the air, water, or soil by human actions. Exhaust fumes from cars are a form of air pollution.

pressure A pressing force.

radioactive Giving off a dangerous form of energy.

reptile An animal such as a lizard or snake that has leathery skin and usually lays eggs.

resin A substance that oozes from some trees and other plants.

rock A solid made from different minerals.

sedimentary rock Rock formed when sand, mud, minerals, or plant and animal remains are pressed together until they harden.

trace fossil The remains of a footprint, burrow, poop, or other sign of an animal, rather than of the animal itself.

translucent Allowing light to pass through, but not able to be seen through clearly.

transparent Able to be seen through clearly.

ultraviolet light Light rays that are beyond the violet end of the spectrum and that cannot be seen by the human eye.

Index